FALLING INTO GRACE

LAURA APOL

Printed in the United States of America.

Dordt College Press
498 Fourth Avenue NE
Sioux Center, Iowa 51250

ISBN: O-932914-42-X

Several of these poems and essays have originally
appeared in various forms and are reprinted with
permission from the following:

The Banner
Christianity and Literature
English Journal
The Hiram Poetry Review
Insight
Sistersong: Women Across Cultures
Urbanite 3
With

Contents

to my parents, Dallas and Gladys Apol
and my children, Jesse and Hanna

PLACES YOU CAN GET LOST

Errant

Winters,
when we needed bread (fresh)
for supper, I was sent.
"Hurry" was my mother's only word.

I slid the dollar in my mitten,
curved my fist around it.
As I walked,
my fingers played its pleated edges
till it (creased and crumpled)
rested on the bakery counter.

After, there was change to carry
and of course the one soft loaf.
Her word and hunger
should have sped me;

still, I dawdled:

day's darkened edges,
warmth of fresh bread,
and a few coins jingling
—loose—
inside my mitten.

Hanging Laundry

There you are, thick waisted,
whistling as you bend-reach,
reach-bend, the swell of your notes
fitting the sheets' cotton curve
in the breeze.

From the window
I see you, gifted at last,
at dance in a world you design—
towels in rows, diapers bleached white,
socks matched.

Bowed over the basket, you become beauty:
the moment aflame,
very ground holy,
sun hot with promise,
clothes sweet and damp.

Line by line you dance on,
pairing cotton and paisley, denim and twill.
Your song rises, falls: infinite grace—
bright as the blouse you hold,
clear as this day's cloudless sky.

Spring Quilting

I am returning your book on quilts. The pattern
I had in mind will wait for another season—
spring has arrived.

Now I will piece together hours of children:
a patchwork of cookies, ice cream and berries,
a bright kite threaded through new leafing trees.

I will pin rows of towels to the clothesline,
edge the drive with snap dragons,
stitch marigolds along the front walk.
I will border the day with birdsong, turning under
the patterns of light.

I will arrange words into samplers of sound:
Irish Chain, Morning Star, Gypsy Trail,
Clay's Choice.

And when I sleep, I will not sleep
on a feather heart pillow; instead,
I will gather my damp-earth dreams,

and, one by one, embroider
a sky full of stars.

On Turning Thirty

This is not a body a man can get lost in—
all planes and hard places, edges.
No trace of the full round
cycles of the moon here;
no hint of the soft curve of sound
women bear in their very name.

Oh, there are places you can get lost:
some mornings there is the late summer song
of a marching band, rehearsing,
and having rehearsed creating music
that draws thought to rhythm and step.
You can get lost in the beat of a band.

And this yard is sunny with dandelions,
busy with bees. The baby
toddles from blossom to blossom,
away from my side and my sight.
You can get lost in a field of humming yellow.

You can get lost in the accumulation
of laundry, the dishes, the dust; lost in phone calls,
junk mail, rice casseroles, tin foil.
Lost in prayer, in thought, in song,
or song and dance.

But you cannot get lost in this body.

Still, she is becoming an old friend,
with her pointed elbows, bony wrists,
too-sharp chin. There is a stride
we've learned together: a breathing,
a pulse—blood and lungs, muscle and bone.
I've known her swollen with child,
aching after a long morning run,
spent beneath a willow.

This is not a body a man can get lost in,
but she holds her own surprises—
comfortable ones, like a new star born
in a familiar sky. And some days,
this old friend feels smooth inside my skin,
almost young, flowing like water.

Failing

You left this morning in a rush, no time for a kiss in the doorway,
our last moments taken with snow pants—
the new ones I promised last winter
but didn't deliver for almost a year.

Out the door on your father's heels, you remembered the lunch
you'd asked me to make, the lunch I'd forgotten, the lunch I promised
—yes, promised since it was my fault for forgetting—
to bring to you by noon.

It was a cheese sandwich on wheat; slices of orange, peeled;
yogurt and a cookie. And this afternoon, when I looked, it was still
on the table, the shiny box bright with reproach.

What did you think, waiting for lunch,
waiting for a mother who promised, waiting for more than a sandwich
—waiting for me at last to remember, to think of you,
to put into your hands what you wished for
—sweet sections of oranges, a circle of cookie—

you my firstborn watching the school door as the clock's hands climbed
to the top of the hour and the class lined up and you asked at last
if they could still count you for hot lunch.

This is not the first time I failed: the day I didn't pick you up
and they phoned for hours before they found your father to bring you home.
The softball games I missed, left you sitting on the bench
as I drove away;

the days I chose words—even my own—over you and your
endless questionings; the songs I let you sing alone, the prayers for you
I never said.

Son, all my mending for you unravels;
the breads I bake never rise and you eat them anyway;
our duets leave me fumbling at the keyboard.
You bring home seeds in a styrofoam cup, pick flowers from the edge
of the neighbor's yard, pretend not to care when I kill them all.
Afterward, you take them out with the trash.

When you are older you will know what I mean when I say
I'm sorry. For now, I will watch from the window
as you walk home from school, careful not to mention the lunch,
chatting instead about friends you saw, books you read, the homework
you don't have.

You are wearing your new snowpants;
they hiss and swish as you move, sigh
as you drop your pack in the house and gather your sled.

On yesterday's meager snow you are sliding away,
down the slope from the house, learning the cold of this day,
your breath releasing in steamy white puffs,
your own hands pushing beside you as you go.

❧

"They are conflicts I have chosen"

(from a conversation with Madeleine L'Engle)

After her presence has reminded me
of everything I thought I should forget,
I walk through cold dark   to home
and a pair of red mittens, waiting to be mended.

And I sigh.

Because, of course, I have not forgotten.

And there is nothing artistic in mending mittens.

Except that these are Mickey Mouse mittens,
and that's alliteration;
they are red as a winter cardinal,
and that's a simile;
they fit hands that I cherish,
which must be symbolic.

And my clumsy needle tugging the thread
is really the incarnation of love,
which, after all, is art.

Sidelines

It is soccer season again—my fourth soccer season, now that my son has begun the fourth grade. I wish I could say that these years have allowed the two of us to grow into soccer, a sport too new to have been part of my elementary years. I wish I could say that I have learned the game. But the truth is that I am only newly understanding terms like wings, keepers and throw-ins. Most of the time that I've spent on the sidelines at practices and games has been busy with my other child, the child who was an infant when her brother first took to the field.

She was six months old that first season in Iowa, and as the autumn chill moved in, I moved with her into our car parked on the sidelines. Usually she napped, soothed by the sun through the car windows, while the young players leaped and flapped to stay warm, their hands pulled up into the sleeves of their jerseys. The games were interminable; only the best players touched the ball and most games ended without either team having scored. In those days, though, time spent on the soccer field was not really about soccer anyway—it was time to burn off energy, time that took restless children onto a wide open space with a ball, a distant goal, and a co-ed team of a dozen.

Now, though, years later and living in Oklahoma, it's different. For one thing, the players have changed. They no longer sit down in the grass when it's their turn to be goalie. They don't tie their shoes mid-play, and they know which goal they should aim toward when they shoot. They keep track of the score now, and the can of soda at the end of the game no longer soothes all losses. They are separated into boys' and girls' teams, they practice twice a week, and often they arrange—and sometimes even win—a mid-week scrimmage against their parents. This is serious business to them now. They've changed.

The parents have changed as well. They don't think these kids are cute anymore. They don't brag when the child hanging by his knees from the goalpost belongs to them. They don't forget whether we're the home or the away team. They don't ask who won at the end of the game; they don't think it's funny when one of our players scores against his own team by mistake. They've changed.

The baby has changed, too. Where once she was content simply to be warm, she has moved with determination through the successive seasons. One year it was all I could do to keep her from crawling off a blanket at practice; the next year I was constantly vigilant to keep her from wandering onto the field during the game. One season I barely watched soccer at all, for she insisted that she and I perform each drill and each play on the sidelines. This year, at last, she is content to watch and to cheer. She has gathered outgrown soccer equipment into her own makeshift uniform, and she is nearly as serious about this game as her older brother and his teammates.

So this is my history on the sidelines of soccer, punctuated as it is by the growth of a young player and the needs of a young child. And it is no wonder that I greet this year with, at last, a sense of relief. My arms are empty, and the time I spend at soccer practice holds the promise of some peace—perhaps a few papers to grade leisurely in the late-afternoon sun, and some quiet reflection sitting in the grass on the sidelines, my daughter at my side. I must confess that my relief is more than a little enhanced by watching a teammate's father as he pushes a stroller to the game and sits with his six-month-old son, rocking and bouncing. I am politely interested, but do not chime in when the other mothers ask if they may hold the baby. Instead, I join the fathers standing near the line at center field and watch the practice proceed.

Until I overhear one of the fathers speak to the father of the baby— the baby who now rests in another woman's arms. "Isn't this a terrific place to bring kids?" the first father inquires, rhetorically it seems, because he goes on, "It's great because there are so many ladies to watch them."

I bristle, but they talk on, introducing themselves by their professions. "I'm a researcher in biology at the University," says the baby's father. "I'm a professor at the law school," says the other man. I want to add that I defended my dissertation in the spring. I want to tell them that I, too, teach, research and write, that I have a life beyond watching children on the sidelines. But before I formulate a response, the mother holding the child approaches, baby in arms. "Michael," she says, addressing the father of the child, "Would you like to scrimmage with the team?" The father hesitates, but the woman holds the baby in my direction. "I'm sure Laura will watch the baby for you," she says.

I am ready to refuse, to remind them of the years I spent with my own infant, toddler, young child on the sidelines. I want to tell them they were exhausted and exhausting years, years without a break, even at a soccer game. I want to say that it is my son's turn to have a mother whose eyes are only for him, a mother who knows which questions to ask, which plays to applaud.

But the father is already stretching his long legs, readying for the game. The baby is thrust into my stiff arms, and I swallow the words.

Sidelines

The baby looks up at me, fusses, squirms a bit, and I walk away, murmuring obligatory words into his hair and bouncing him resentfully in my arms. He curves himself to my rigid shoulder and rests his head.

I tell myself it is not his fault we are here, together, but I am still angry. I am angry because this is my chance—mother or not—to have arms that belong to no one but myself, to be known on the sidelines for who I am, what I do. It is my chance to fill my head with my own thoughts, to watch my son's developing skill, to sit beside my daughter in the grass. This is not my child, this is not my choice, this is not my . . . The baby is asleep. His breathing is deep and peaceful. It is the breathing of all babies; it is the breath of my own children. He is a comfortable weight against my chest. He is warm.

Strangely, I find that my anger has changed; there is a good feeling this baby brings to my arms and I am surprised to realize that he could become my choice after all. He is the moment that reminds me of other moments, he is the link to a time of life that will not come for any of us again.

I see from a distance that my son has scored a goal for his team. It is greeted with much celebration, and he high-fives his teammates. When he looks my way, I give him a smile, and he is pleased. My daughter has made a friend, and they are kicking a ball between them at the other end of the field.

And this contented weight in my arms? He is not a child who will own my days or confuse my nights. He is here, now. Someday soon he will wander onto the field, and I will let his father retrieve him. Someday soon he will kick a ball along the sidelines, and I will let his father return it. For now, though, I will allow myself to enjoy him, sleeping on my shoulder. And I will do this for my own reasons: not because I am a woman, but because we have all—children, players, parents—changed. And because, resting in my arms, this baby reminds me of it.

At the Cove*

We came here the winter your father died,
and again the spring I thought I'd forgotten how to breathe.
There's room here to spread out the fragments

we tote in our shoulder sacks—
our mothers, our marriages, the children
who tie our tongues and own our days.

There's time here for coffee, cup after cup
until our words loosen and race on sure limbs
across fields yet to be planted.

This is, indeed, a cove—shelter from storms,
inlet, gulf; a place to harbor
hurt, anger and doubt. Metal tables and

linoleum floor, hum of fluorescent lights
and vinyl seats the color of tangerines—these are real.
Farmers in seed-corn caps and striped

bib overalls are real. Wives in polyester prints
are real. Shell-pink carnations in dime-store vases—
they're real as well. So are the tides

of duty, dreams sucked like sand
from beneath our feet, and the bedrock of friendship
keeping our lives at bay.

*The Cove is a restaurant along Interstate 80 between
    Davenport and Iowa City, Iowa.

Weaning the Baby

All day my body has hungered for her,
more, it seems, than she for me,
her interest consumed by her own chubby legs,
star-shaped hands that clutch the cup,
her own self now everything,
explosive consonants to say she is becoming child.

Yet I resist, swelling breasts taut
and whole body throbbing for
the yeasty smell of her still sweet,
mewling cries and round pink mouth, pink tongue,
warm curved hand.

The turn of her body was once all toward me;
now it is all away.

But in dark, through rising drift of dreams,
she wakes knowing want, knowing hunger
for comfort, milk-rich. It is enough for me
to nurse that need, to nurse once more
that small tugging need.

On Waking, Four a.m.

When I stirred tonight it was just that
I dreamed of a sound at the door,
a slight sound, really—

some other door perhaps, swinging
on its hinges, the chiming of a distant
clock tower in the dark, or someone

rising nearly noiselessly to
bank the embers of the night's low fire.
It was only a dream, though, just the house

settling for a few final hours.
I could have settled as well, my bones
sinking back to the cove of this bed.

But my thoughts roused
and I rose to find paper and pen.
Here I am, hushed with longing, huddled

close to a dim light, trusting one breath of
this night, one frame of this faint dream,
to these quietly wandering words.

Spring Settling

And now you are eyeing the coast, longing
to taste that Pacific surf, roaring
—raw power and coffee shops on the
pier where they grind their own
hazelnut beans.

Such is the primordial impulse, all
surge and spray. I've been safe stream,
swimmer, mother's milk; never surf,
salty waves, never brine-tainted
ocean cafe.

But you claim you could settle
for ponds on the plains, swollen with
spring. Brook, creek, April's pale
compromise I will not be.
While you think of settling,

Watch for me: wind-driven,
sudden as prairie fire,
washing like tides across sand.

Moving to Oklahoma

1

Brittle as this late-August grass in
damn-it's-hot-Oklahoma,
rain is what I wish not to find but to be—
part of sky / air / sea

washing the space between earth
and heaven, soaking into
rust-red soil and yes, thank God,
welcome.

2

That my life has turned over and
over like a rolling hoop
does not mean that anything
has changed.

3

When I say *life* what I mean
is *location*—the where of being.

I have seldom seen broader sunsets
or deeper sunrises;
I have rarely noted so fully each
phase of the moon.

It is all distance, ache and ease
growing side by side
with each moment's deep breath

in this far far place.

4
The telephone lines
go somewhere, and they are
studded with loud birds who fly
where they will. I would be like
those birds, noisy with choice

—birds whose feet tingle
each time my distant dreams
call.

❦

Line of Symmetry

He learned it today in second grade, and at
supper he can hardly wait to explain: *it divides
everything exactly in half, Mom.* The line

of symmetry. It is folded paper—red—and the
ice cream cones I used to cut out to make hearts
that were even and round and met at a perfect point.

Like that girl with the scissors, he believes life has,
life is, a mirror image—cross sections of oranges,
the curved sound holes at the waist of a violin.

Theirs is faith in perfection, hers and his,
a place where identical halves make a whole
and everything fits. I want to tell them

about jagged edges, lines of agony, halves
that never will match. I want to show them
the cutouts I've made imperfectly, points

off center, folded lines slipping—my own life
a study of mismatch and imbalance, red heart
after red heart.

But for now I let them believe—son and
young self poised in a still-perfect world where,
scissors in hand, they become

mirror images of one another.

Lemon Meringue

In the end, what we will owe the world
is a lemon meringue pie—both sweet and tart,
all our successes and failures

gelled in translucent filling
and the juice of lemons squeezed one by one
into a cup that is never filled.

Taste this. It is life poured into a pre-baked crust
patterned with fork-pricks that name our days.
If we have done anything right,

it was that Sunday of song, rain and a warm stove.
If we have done anything wrong,
it was the pie we threw away,

the pie that didn't measure up.
Tell me again how meringue, whipped just so,
forms lofty peaks. That is the part that lies ahead—

the future, the someday we keep owing the world

like a sweet white debt.

WINGS FOLDED
CLOSE TO THE HEART

On the Night of the First Snow

You were born in the month
of your father, grandfather,
and great-grandfather,
on the night of the first snow.

As outside, whiteness covered
stained, scarred fields,
in you the fourth generation met life
with newly opened eyes.

Ten fingers and ten toes
(your mother counted)
soon wrapped in fleeced white
you seemed the soft breath of perfection.

Your mother held you, wept,
unfolded your clenched fist,
watched snowflakes melt against
the dark window.

Bonding

Birth
Newborns bond to smell
—blood and sweat—as we hold them,
still wet, near our breasts, lead their soft mouths
to the nipple. They know—they already know—
what to do.

It is our bond, this flesh, this scent,
this milk that is not milk at all
but a prelude. They know us by smell, by touch;
they know us by taste and we
are not all the same.

Heredity
These are the gifts of mothers to daughters—
gifts we wear for a lifetime. Blessings,
curses, too large or too small. Men
eye them, joke about them, brush against them,

tell us women are alike in the dark. Here, then,
is a difference: my grandmother's breasts
were the family treasure, hoarded, laced tightly
into corsets, bound by stiff brassieres.
She gave her daughter half the gift,
who passed even less to me.

I have a nice smile. Beautiful eyes.
They rarely count in the dark.

The Race
Three thousand women on a hot
Sunday morning, racing for a cure—
women striding across miles for their bodies,
for the bodies of their mothers,
for their friends, lovers and sisters,
for their daughters.

I, too, am running: for my daughter,
barely four months, who waits at the finish.
For my mother, who has recently learned
that her cysts are benign. And for myself—
this shape I have learned
not to love, but to live with.

I am running because I am a woman.

Three miles later my legs ache, but not so much
as my throbbing breasts—breasts that let down
as I hear her cry above the noise of the crowd,
mixing once more warm milk, hot sweat and
my own smell.

She takes it hungrily.

Weaning
How gently we reclaim our bodies,
slip a finger between the lip and nipple,
breaking the seal. We do it at each feeding;
we do it one last time at weaning.

I nursed the youngest well into her first year
because she would be the last,
because these breasts would not know another.

How I mourned that last feeding, that last
insistent tug;

how I savored that last thread of milk,
drawn from the space near my heart.

First Flight: For Jesse

For years I have left you at thresholds—
walked you to the edge of the pool on the first day
of lessons, stood outside the door
your first day of school.

This is a mother's life, this nudge
of love and fear and relief in one deep breath.
Like fish swimming against the water's flow,
you have fought and floated,
I have hurried and held.

Today was another rite in this journey.
I left you at the boarding gate,
watched you in too-short jeans (four inches you
shot up this summer) hand the flight attendant
your ticket.

No last kiss for me, no hug—
a smile of eight-year-old bravado and a long look
were all I took from the airport as your plane
became a smudge in God's eye.

Storms over St. Louis have grounded you indefinitely
though the sky above those clouds is filled with stars.
I know you will see them;
for you the holy dancer's veils will part
and the moon will welcome your fledgling self
as I would.

Jesse, each star has a name
and dreamers have wished on them since time began.
If, white knuckled, you wish I were there,
know I am waiting as always outside the door—
here on the far side of the clouds,

praying God breathes gently tonight,
praying God breathes gently for you.

candling

after her husband died she candled eggs:

ivory ovals held to the flame, translucent,
my beautiful dark-haired grandmother
spinning smooth shells between her
beautiful fingers, cradling them gently
near the heat, reading the stories
beneath the brittle skin

my grandmother packing the good eggs with care,
discarding the others in a steel pail

my grandmother taking the baby with her to work
listening to him cry while she bent to her task
fifteen brief minutes to nurse him
in the hot glare of the other women's eyes

my grandmother, wood crate of eggs before her
working the night shift, more eggs, another flat,
hands stained with chicken dung, nails broken,
gagging at the ripe yellow stench, more eggs

my grandmother, hair turning, hands bleeding,
picking dirty eggs from straw,
holding them to the scrutiny of fire

seeing beneath the shells the shadow of her dreams,
dropping them into the bucket at her feet.

Pieces of Love: Jeanette Apol Ruis

My grandmother's recent letter ended with these words: "Do you need more blankets? I guess not—I've given away so many no one wants any more." The voice behind the words seemed sad, and I wanted to call her and say, "Oh yes, send a blanket. The nights are cold and we need another quilt." But it was summer and the few beds in our home were already covered. So I didn't phone.

Still, the longer I thought, the more I wanted to tell her what has become of her quilts—the way they grace our beds and have for years; the squares of fabric I recognize from her closets, or from my mother's, or from my own; the stories that are stitched into the squares—this blanket made for my wedding, this one for the baby's crib, this one because the holes in the sofa needed a cover. I wanted to tell her about taking home newborns in blankets she has knitted, baptizing children in shawls edged with her crochet, moving toddlers to a big bed in a new room in a different city—a bed covered with a spread she pieced. I wanted to tell her that her quilts have shaped the dreams of those who slept under them; that we gave a blanket we had outgrown to the Kurdish refugees the winter of the war; that sometimes I wander through the house late at night, tucking a son or a daughter under her quilts. I wanted to tell her about the blankets I have set away for my children and for their children yet to be born, and I wanted to promise never to pass on a quilt without telling the story of the woman who made it.

The story I will tell is this: there was a woman who, young, was left alone with children and land and possessions and debt, like so many ragged pieces of cloth. Bit by bit she fit them together, sometimes at great personal cost, seeing patterns form in the scraps, creating designs where they seemed not to have been. She started at the center, piecing, sewing with great faith—stitching into it her many jobs, finding people to care for her young children, taking the baby with her to work. Bit by bit her quilt began to take shape: meeting another man she grew to love; fitting his family into the design and fitting herself to his family; working beside him for years, still stitching, still stitching until all the children were grown, with children of their own, and cancer took him, and she was piecing alone again after all those years. But there were grandchildren to love and to guide into the fabric, and the blanket kept growing until it was bigger than she had ever imagined, more than she had ever dreamed standing in her kitchen that day so long ago, looking at her table, looking at her hands, looking at four children and a bare field.

Pieces of Love

When I hand my children their quilts, I will tell them the story of a woman who has never stopped stitching, piecing, knitting lives to her own with love—a woman whose hands have never been still. I will show them the way the scraps of fabric fit together, the patterns that repeat, the bits of yarn, pulled through, tied tight, that hold it all together. I will tell them that these are her gifts to us: gifts to keep us warm; gifts to celebrate marriage and birth and growth and even death; gifts that grace our homes, cover our needs, welcome our guests; gifts that say love to the homeless and peace to the war-torn.

Her gifts are more than she knows. If she asks me again if we need more quilts, I will tell her the truth: of course we do.

Living with M.S.

Living with M.S.
is like the moment you step off the merry-go-round
and the whole world is spinning, and you are not,
but really it is only you.
It is a race between your tongue and your brain
with no winner;
it is dancing on marbles
with a cup of hot coffee, too full.

Living with M.S.
is writing your name under water.
It is a hill so long you barely know it happens
until you turn around and see where you've been.
You pull your family in a wagon the color of hope;
your grandson watches you stumble, cries if you fall.
You go on.

Living with M.S.
happens to everyone you love, to everyone who loves you.
On a bad day—even on a good day—
it leaves you on your knees.
Sometimes you call it pain; sometimes its name
is grace.

❧

For my Father

Outside this window, the light is reclaiming itself
and the wind presses so hard the snowflakes rise:
God, how I wish it were so.

I have been told she was once the life of the party,
and she was. Some days I see that spark.
How I mourn the woman I hardly knew.

Could it not have been fifteen years,
twenty strong years, twenty-five,
and then something   something swift
—the heart pausing mid stroke,
one red flower blooming wild in the brain?

As it is, we are always sweeping
but never sweeping up,
driving through an all-day rain,
searching for some lightening of the clouds.

Here it is, at last,
the poem we have been writing for her all our lives.

When can we stop pretending we are whole?

Holding the Moon

I would give it to him, the blond boy
perched on the hood of his father's black '39 Chevy,
eyes squinting into day's stark sun but

dreaming the moon even then,
arms aching to hold and be held in its soft light,
waiting for all life's promises to be kept.

Yes, I would give it to him—
the moon and more than the moon if I could.
I would keep those half-said promises,

turned silky with the passing years,
keep all the magic words,
chant them over and over to him in the dark,

remind him that love's cycles are indeed like the moon,
the inexplicable face of the moon, pulling us all,
and rising.

Without Failing

Say the parachute always opens, the rope
on the rock's steep face never snaps;

say your fingers never fumble on the
Brandenburg and the wind always fills

your sails. Say your words spill onto the
page without effort, your brush dances palette

to canvas with ease. Say you sing that song, skate
that fine-edged skate, sink the three point shot.

Say mile twenty-six feels as good as
mile thirteen, the water beneath the cliff

is deep enough for your dive, your skis know
the ridge of the mountain and the coral reef opens itself

to your eager eyes. Say he answers the phone this time, and
imagine this: he loves you, he loves you,

he loves you
like an open yellow-centered daisy.

Long Run

I don't want to run
unless it is dark,
the lake rising up to the road and
the frogs' notes
braided like a rag rug.

I don't want to run
unless the moon is a narrow gash
in the west
and Orion has completed
his cartwheel through the sky.

I don't want to run
unless the slope is gentle
and the pavement is smooth
as night's breath
and your stride beside me fits

and the road goes on
and on

On Returning Home for Thanksgiving and Running Into an Old Love

I grew up in a room with raspberry curtains,
and you were there, the one my parents hated
and could not say for fear I would live forever
with a choice I made young.
If I had my way we would meet again
on a beach with no moon.
I would be as always your safe harbor.

As if safety made life sweet and dreams were
the color of fresh berries.
The stairs to my bedroom were steep,
and on each step I told you a story
that lasted one thousand nights.

Outside, snow is falling and I have barely time
to thank God I trimmed my hair
before you are summoned by my thoughts
or I by yours. Our bones have not forgotten.
All the words we thought but never said
crowd to the edges of our talk:
fine weather, home for the holidays,
remember making love under the willows?
Why did we not choose each other?

Mornings, I would wake to brew coffee
as if we cared. And perhaps we did—
that one red geranium blooming in the window
and the smell of fresh coffee, poured.

Pulses

The wind presses, pulls
    sucks warmth from leafless shadows
        beyond our window
    drifts through cracks, rifts
        in these walls
            —across my bared shoulder,
                the side of your face
You sleep on;
    your blood thuds heavy, warm
        steady beneath my ringed hand

Anniversary

All day they prayed for rain
the clean stroke of lightning
the rage of thunder.
as if after fifty years they could be
anything but what they knew

His dark suit too hot for July
her full-skirted scarlet too bright
he once said he loved red   long ago

Fifty years they waited
for rain of one sort or another:
weathered droughts, lean years,
the deluge of children they did not want
and could not afford.

fifty years she has harbored the weight of his silence;
fifty years he has silenced the rush of her words

They sigh, stand together,
endure friends gathering like clouds in the closed churchyard,
pose, smiling into the blinding flashes.
Congratulations.

Years have pulled them far from what they were.
always she has walked in the eye of the storm;
always he has watched from the porch

The rain at last breaks on them, quick and fierce
cleaving the long, hot day.
The dark suit is soaked, the dress ruined.

lightning does, in fact, strike the same place twice
they have known it, time and again

She turns her face to the wind.

He starts toward home.

❦

Living with a Vegetarian

It is, at last, not fish or chicken but red meat
that catches his eye, a bloody three pound
rump roast—ruby red—that leads him astray.

He was not raised for denial
(couscous and whole wheat, zucchini and sprouts)
and once she, too, loved sirloin, ham steak,
pork chops and ribs.

Where were the clues, those hints
of the turns life would take?

Now he learns the butcher's first name,
buys beef while she's away—roasts it slowly,
lovingly basting, saving the drippings
for gravy. No potatoes.
No sliced bread or salad or pie.
Just slices of meat, slabs really,
tender and marbled with fat.

He eats in one sitting, pound after pound,
with a fervor he thought forgotten.
Each forkful is protest, each mouthful
his well-done revenge.
The aroma lingers for days.

She says nothing. There is nothing to say:
that platter of beef, roasted tender, tinged pink
is his love—past and future. Its succulent juice
curbs his craving, slakes deeper hungers
than she has for years.

Private Geographies

When someone asks *why*, for a moment
I see your face, the light in your eyes,
the moon rising—whole—through trees October to
August and all the winter, spring, summer between.

Stirred by that asking, choice rustles brittle and stark
in the autumn wind.

This, too, is history—louder than wars, protests and
proclamations, all our moments locked
into rocks by the water's edge, floodwaters receded at last.

Would we still know this place?

—country roads laid square mile by mile, corners
sharp, angles right. Somewhere along this tireless grid
the blurred shape of a pond waits in a hollow,
fish flashing silver, here and here.

This is less place than story: woman, man, cleft of chin,
curve of thigh, plain furrow arch—as if for a moment
insistent time's passage made us soft enough
to be shaped.

Would we still know this place?

It is all new: new moon, new season, new water's path.
New roads now, new choices,

new me.

Mending

The day we parted, when the future was simply
a gash in our lives and the past was a series
of frayed edges,

that day we did not kiss one last time.
We did not wash the sheets,
mop the floors, take out the trash

or phone our friends. We did the mending.
Our daughter's sweater needed a button,
our son's pants had a loose seam.

You sat at the machine,
I picked up a needle and thread and,
across the table where we'd shared

so many meals, we stitched—
as always, your stitches tight, even, sure,
mine loose and haphazard.

Still, there is something to be said for mending
on such a day:

there is the wisdom of knowing which things
can be salvaged;

there is the art of choosing the right stitch.

Sinfonia for Strings

After goodbye, tuning is everything: these strings home
beneath my fingers—old friends, their sound, their feel.
Touch them; they are music waiting to be played. Press fingers
here, and here: it is this Sinfonia—Telemann—

that knits me together this morning, these clean rhythms,
these weaving notes I have followed so much of my life,
my fingers gathering up edges without effort—crossing,
pressing, climbing strings, changing pitch with motion.

Kiss me a yes, I hear in the space between sustained notes in the
opening line, the line that erases itself and never repeats,
and suddenly all is melody. Hands forget what they've known,
move only in these notes, this asking of instrument,

this resonance drowning all others. Music lives in the body
and this is what the heart knows: even in the deep
water hums, desire the siren's song like a thread, pulling.
I would trade my soul for a braided rope, lash my back to the mast.

But no—here I am, no twine but the twining of melody,
graceful as limbs singing through water:
Telemann, prelude and postlude, left hand bridging
the strings, right arm bowing for life, whole body

leaning, bobbing, knowing Telemann as never before,
Telemann pressed into service, crisscrossed into safety:
scaffold, net, raft, buoy, *Sinfonia. Sinfonia.* Upbow,
downbow. Play on.

White Paper Tablecloths

Were there flowers on the tables? Candles?
I only remember tall ceilings, wood chairs,
olive oil, and wine in a glass gallon jug—

cold, cold wine that went down like water.
Fresh ground pepper, hot bread and words
edged with garlic—your voice and mine.

And there were old loves: men we'd broken, mostly
men who had broken us, letters we still needed
to write. *I've been saving a kiss for a long time*

I said. *Bastard* was your response.
We hated them, mourned them, poured two more
tumblers of blush zinfandel. No hurry:

anger keeps if you bank the fire just so;
we'd had practice. No dessert, thanks,
just more wine. When the waiter—blond,

blue-eyed boy—touched my blouse, the look I gave
held all the rage, all the sadness we'd traded for food.
He didn't return, but we left him a big tip

because all the men we'd lost had blue eyes.
Flowers or candles? Just the white paper
tablecloth mattered at last:

we emptied our glasses, gathered the check,
and wrote on the sheeting: *Thanks Tim.*
For everything. We didn't sign our names.

New Year's Day

It's an old poem, really: a lake and a wooden
dock and the children, blonder than either of us
and happy. If I could choose beginnings—

the first note played by a lone violin or the flake
that touches our bones at the threshold of snow—
if I could name those breaths,

I would name them here, name them now.
Bread on the water, and a single gull, circling,
and then, like the crowding of days we have shared,

twenty or sixty, a hundred or more.
Sunset blazes behind us, gulls dipping and rising like waves,
breasts gilded with sun's flame.

Their glow is no richer, is no more refined
than the light in our daughter's rare smile
or the deep knowing eyes of our son.

This is the melding of passage: fire and water,
bread from the dock, and the year's first day closing
like wings folded close to the heart.

THIS BURNING CIRCLE
OF DREAMS

Cabin

—for Stephanie

Imagine we are there, no sound but our own breathing,
no words but the words we choose. Which are the first words?
Do we speak of trees opening, the white-lipped edge of the lake—
dreams we have grown into, even late in our dreaming lives?

Imagine there are silences and we don't need to fill them;
imagine when the lake calls we follow, slip into water
the way we slip into our own selves—so rarely, but with such joy.

Imagine we have no worries, no other lives knocking at the door,
no gardens growing out of control while we sleep.
Only trees we have never seen before, never touched.
Even the sky is new, ours for these moments.

Imagine that finally I have words for how you have saved me—
what you took me from, what you took me to.

Imagine that the sunsets, moonrises, meteor showers do not tell us
time is passing, days are slipping through our fingers like sand.
Instead, let them say that our lives are a circle—
twined, intertwined, inseparable.

Running with Wolves

How do you know when you find them,
these women who run with the wolves? Is it
the blaze in their fierce eyes, their lean strong
thighs, or their sides, singed from
carrying fire?

See how gently they have learned to
reclaim their bodies: noiseless stride,
pause, and then straightening
to shake the wind from their
tangled hair.

I would be one of them, across fields
stained with snow, tracking a brilliant
sliver of moon. Here is my torch—
this burning circle of dreams.
My howl echoes deep in the night sky.

A Red Feather

Last night, Susan, I dreamed you had come back
and had come back to me,
and the skirt I once helped you choose
had not faded, was still cobalt blue.

There were trees where we stood,
trees tall as light,
and I was happy just to watch you
and tell you that now it is me
trying to hold things together.

You know what I mean.

If it hadn't been so dark around the edges
we might have gone on talking
but ladders go up as well as down
and you said your life was working out fine.
You said.

You might have said more if the wind
had not stolen your lines,
if our words had been heavier
than a red feather on a breeze.

As it is, my lips were the shape of I miss you
when the baby cried and, once again,
you were gone.

Sleeping in my Grandmother's Bed

All night the wind cries in the dark with the voice
of the children I have not borne. Awakened,
I cradle the edges of sleep,
nursing the common thread of our dreams.

Your fourth child, my father, was born at the turn of the year.
After daughters, a son was a farmer's rich harvest;
with such an inheritance he purchased land
and prepared it for planting.

But the wind and cold rains caught in his lungs,
made you a widow by spring.
If the child had not been a son,
you would not be alone.

You buried your choice:
sold the farm, moved the family, worked. Mostly worked.
Your story was one child too many—
a thought you could not bring to words.

Until now. In the darkness,
our voices have claimed us as women,
weaving for hours what has been taken.
Our breathing in sleep's flight mixes as if we were one.

You who have passed along life and the rhythms of life,
our lives are now sounded against silent passage.
Outside, the night cries in the dark like a child, like a male child;
the story that shapes us is shaped by the force of the wind.

Passage

Tonight, Grandfather, I wanted most
to be with you, to hold your hand and stay
as you walk through the shadows.

Instead, I'm walking the floor with this
bawling bundle, pacing the clock as I would have
there, in the room of your rattling breath.

Yet I'm nearer than you know, here with
my son, and tonight he dreams your memories.
You speak a shared language—

his the mystery of learning;
yours, of unlearning. He grabs life greedily,
with both hands; I can't keep you

from giving it to him.

Every First Apple

I am standing on the empty lot that was once my grandparents' house, my mother's home. It is a field now, with tall grass that sweeps along the hem of my red skirt, brushing my legs with cool damp strokes. It is autumn. The scent of apples from the trees at the back of the field fills the air as it has for so many seasons. Standing here is like relearning lines from an almost-forgotten piece of music: sometimes there are silences, spaces not easily filled; sometimes the memories rush in like the sweep of a melody, line over line.

I am tired from the drive and the afternoon sun, but the earth is warm beneath my bared feet. I traveled by car to this town—past fields of ripe corn and the harvest of beans—but, arriving, I wanted to walk, knowing there are things that need to be measured and paced. I wanted to fit my stride to the past, to place my feet in the tracks of my mother, in the steps of my grandmother.

As I stepped from the car, I slipped off my sandals. The bite of gravel, sharp in the warm sand, cut into my soles, but I didn't walk the hard lanes pressed in the dirt. Instead, I chose the loose shoulder, the part graded and leveled and smoothed with each season. My footsteps, stretching behind me, were deep and evenly spaced.

To my left was the cemetery—a shelter of trees and a black metal fence. I turned on the path near the gate. It was cool under the trees, shaded from the bright September sky. At first I couldn't find the spot—I hadn't been there since winter. I had driven through quickly that time, merely stayed for my grandfather's funeral. Now I walked slowly but recognized nothing in eight months' growth.

The bare, upturned earth startled me. I thought my loss had healed; yet here it was, fresh as the clods of dark soil, new as the cuts of his name in granite. I knelt, brushed the dirt from his stone with my skirt, placed my hand on the green sod beside him (a reminder of how long we'd been without Grandma) and remembered the corn fields we'd walked through each autumn. Now I wished I could show this old farmer the drying stalks in the fields and stand by his side as he stripped back the husks.

Silently, as I walked into town, the sky turned from cobalt to pink to stone gray. In the half-light I came to this lot, and now I am standing on land that was theirs. The crickets shrill in the damp grass, and the night air is filled with the sweet smell of apples. To the north, the Dipper hangs low, laden with Indian Summer and the promise of autumn.

Every First Apple

Over there, where the dip in the grass reaches the road, was the shed. And right here, I am standing in my grandma's kitchen, with a white tiled floor that was waxed and rewaxed. "No running!"—I hear her speak clearly, and see myself, slippered, slide from the doorway, across that linoleum, to stop near the stove. In those days I slept in the cold bedroom upstairs, but at nap times I lay on Grandma's bed. "Blessed are the pure in heart, for they shall see God"—a black square hung on the wall, and I traced the words on the bedspread when they thought I was sleeping.

The breeze in the field has turned chilly. I walk from the house—this fresh-seeded grass—to the tall willow tree in the back. Here's where we laid blankets, made grocery stores, restaurants, and homes. The branches touched the ground then; we parted them to enter, watched them close behind us. And Grandpa, sitting on the steps behind the house, made whistles—chose the wood, cut and skinned and carved it smooth.

The night is getting colder. Before I go, I have one last thing to see: the apple trees. The limbs are thick and heavy with pink fruit tinged with a darker blush of ripeness. These are the first apples of the season, sweetly sour—the kind that pull with a pleasurable pain at the soft hollows just behind the ears. Once we would have filled bushel baskets with these apples; we would have carried them between us to the house. Now I reach out, stroke the smooth, tight skins, and wonder why no one has pruned and picked these trees: the fruit is ready to make sauce, I hear my grandpa say.

I choose the largest apple in the darkness, and as I turn I rub its skin against my cotton skirt. I look back from the road, feel once more the silence and the spaces, turn the apple in my hand, then bite. The polished skin is smooth against my lips. The fruit is not yet ripe; the juice is sweetly tart and, as always, makes me wince. It is everything, yet nothing I expected it would be: it is every first apple.

How To Write a Poem

Once you can hear the circles closed inside each tree
tell a different story, you are ready. When you notice
the house breathe in the dark, there is no going back:
swing open the gate, let memory enter
with the hot ring of truth.

> A woman unfolds with your words; she steps into
> the house you are building, nudges the porch swing
> with her bare foot. She is listening.

> *Long ago you placed a coin in your dead father's*
> *fist to remind him of a boy who lived*
> *for the sweetness of applesauce—a boy who knew*

> *not only the fruit of the trees but the trees themselves:*
> *their curved bridges, weighted branches, and the*
> *windfalls beneath, humming with hornets.*

> *All your father loved he found in that boy's blue eyes,*
> *even the defiance that pitched bruised fruit at the barn*
> *when the task was raking and gathering. It was never enough;*

> *one more wheelbarrow always waited to be pushed through the woods,*
> *far past the fence, to the creek-edged entrance of Whiskey Cave.*
> *The scent of fermenting apples was pungent as moonshine.*

> *Now moonshine lets you see change in the almost-round*
> *orb in the sky, bright as a dime,*
> *touched like a fallen woman.*

> It is late: the fire has burned low, dawn is crackling
> at night's edge. Near you someone still listens,
> hearing shapes in your songs.

Writing the poem: the house breathes around you, quiet inhale
and exhale, deep wordless sighs. Not this night, but some other
you will know that this is the art: a listener, a story—
what is said in the dark after midnight
is always a poem.

Late Night Call

Tonight yours was the last
voice I heard, yours were
the tones that stroked
my dreams into color.

This is sweet, this sleep
gleaming

—like the ice-thickened limbs
of the back yard elm

another year crackling under
that frozen weight,

—like the glazed telephone wires
humming with voices,

words pulsing beneath their
cool cool cool skin.

Copying Poems

If I am going to send you poems in exchange
for more poems, I would rather the poems were my own—
my music weaving your dreams.

I would rather it was I who gave you
the certainty of supper flavored with words,
I who gathered flowers with colors you could taste and smell,
I who pulled back the curtains to charm the moon each night.

Even the new moon.
Even a starless night.

But where I walk snow is falling,
the sky unfolding its petals of silence.
Another poet says it better—*snow and flowers,*
flowers and snow—so I stand here, alone, under bright light,
in a place that promises safe ways to reproduce words and dreams,
to share supper and flowers, moonlight and snow.

Here, then, are the pages you wanted—poems you marked,
poems that marked you. And here on the edge is my lone
hand, printed over and over, faithfully
holding the pages in place.

Crossing

If I had not wept, seated as I was at the window
over the jet's wing on that early morning flight

if I had not packed fear in my bruised Samsonite,
bound it with a stretch of cotton clothesline
then lugged it through the airport and onto
the waiting bus

if you had not been there to lead me onto the ferry
with its wide wall of windows, its rows of plastic seats
and its open decks—been there to remind me
of stories that open to the slight nudge of our voices
like evening rain over the Sound

if we had not stood with damp night wind in our hair

if we had not chosen words over warmth,
words over the chowder they served below,
words over everything but breathing
and sometimes even over that

if we had not been talking for our lives, covering years
with swift strokes of the tongue

if listening had not fed us

Then I would have remembered to open my sack,
take out the camera I'd tucked there hours before

I would have remembered to focus the lens
the very moment the clouds cleared and, for an instant,
we were beautiful and smiling in moonlight

suspended, as we were, between lands,
our lives like a ferry,
crossing.

Orange

We might carve our names in the bridge's secret place
if we knew we could return to read the story of our own lives.

Instead we trace the rim of the lake in the pale afternoon sun.

The buds hold their breath.

No one asks what we would choose: the white flash of a doe,
or a blackbird's flame-tipped wing. No one offers us tomorrow
and so we take, hungrily, sunset on a wooden dock
and one last orange to share—

your hands turning it over and over,

and that round globe the world glowing like fire.

Waiting for an Eclipse

The eclipse was not seen.
We waited these hours for nothing but light.

The eclipse
—and I take my son to the shop where they cut off his curls
The platinum snippings circle his chair

was
—and I sing to the baby of time and of prayers
and of where we go when we grow up

not
—and the dog dreams of wolves in the dark
and of wild creatures chasing and chased

seen
—and at night we make love because you are here
and the sheets smell like sunshine and wind

The eclipse was not seen.

Except in Hawaii, a six minute shadow
the shape of a full morning moon interrupted the sun.
Six minutes and you can go blind gazing into that fire.

The eclipse was not seen. Or maybe it was.
They claim it is beautiful, bright beyond words.

Near Miss

How near is a near miss?

Think of the poem you almost didn't write,
    the kiss you almost knew was wrong,
    the man you nearly didn't walk with up the mountain.

Think of your children's chromosomes reversed,
    your father the pilot who never came home.
    Imagine the biopsy positive, the letter unopened,
    the apology hoarded too long.

Grace picks her moments with care—
    no chance-filled spin of the wheel, no tossed dice.
    Instead, a touch on the shoulder, a voice too urgent
    for words saying look, look over there. That woman—
    sit there.

How near is a near miss?

I saw the woman. I sat beside her.
    We were not beautiful; there was little to say.
    But she held out a gift grace told me to take
    and weeks later I brushed my hair, wore a plaid jumper
    and sat in a circle of women passing fire through my hands.
    I have sat there ever since.

I am saying this because any moment
    I could have turned right instead of left, I could have hesitated,
    I could have opened the wrong door.

A near miss:
    Change any part of the story
    and you might not have chanted for me the Christmas
    I prayed your names from far away.
    You might not have heard me—made me strong, made me sure,
    made me howl. The wolves might have slept on;
    the seal might never have slipped back into her skin.

How near is a near miss?

Near as fingers that almost didn't meet, lives that almost
passed without touching, voices that almost didn't throw sparks.

Our fingers did meet, our lives touched, our voices caught and flamed.
Think of this: I might not have learned dance. I might not have learned song.
I might not have learned you.

But I did.

class reunion

Old friends,
with you words twist,
a clear plastic straw between stiff fingers.
I try to prove I have not stopped becoming.
Kathy, she dances,
her now graceful body curves currents
I have not felt.
Sue Ellen, she smiles,
speeds beautiful past what I have known.
And I, I remain
white lip of the ocean where
–once in foam–
surf touches sand.

You Told Me They Would Be Purple

This is to account for my silence—letters I've not written
and the phone that never rings by your bed.

In the months since my leaving I have sent messages in other ways:

Late September I planted the tulips you gave,
a black dirt border of longing near the drive.

In October, the piles of leaves I raked
—apple tree, pear, silver maple—raked to blisters
and aching arms, they were my words for you.
And the backyard feeder told my November:
chickadee, cardinal, jay arriving at dawn,
disappearing by noon.

In December, each wide-winged snow angel
was a message to you. January ice
and February tracks along a frozen stream—
they were my letters as winter dragged on, as you, far away,
readied for spring.

The night wind in March carried my dreams
to your door.

And now April. The tulips have spiked their way
early through snow.

Such faith I had, months ago,
that a shoebox of papery bulbs would remember spring.
Such faith that they would find their way.
They are slow tulips—the last on my street
to thicken into buds.

In May, when they open their serrated scent to the sun,
at last I will know what to write:

the tulips remember. They *have* found their way.
And Fran, you were right—

they are purple.

What I Know

I know the familiar ten-mile feel in my legs
at the start of a race. I know the bass line of Corelli's
Christmas Concerto and Pachelbel's Canon in D.
I know white wine, cold beer, hazelnut coffee—black.

I can navigate Kansas City rush hour in the rain. I have
packed my suitcases at midnight and traveled through
dark. I know children's first words and the stories that
follow. My lips know the stain of fresh berries.

I have crossed the Mississippi when its banks
were downtown buildings and farms; I have seen
a double sun dog gracing the sky on a winter day.
I know shooting stars, moss roses, jasmine tea.

I've watched six yellow finches at the feeder at dawn,
I've viewed a solar and a lunar eclipse from the same bridge.
I know how towels stiffen on the line in the summer sun;
I know Oklahoma wind, Iowa cold,

the silence of good byes that are too hard to say.
I once met an angel who entered my second-floor class
through a window. I know grass always forgets,
but trees hold their memories forever.

I know I love dancers and skiers,
and women who know what they know.
And I honor those women who are only beginning
to learn.

Still to Be Said

If my words have, as you once said while you
cradled the cup I offered without cream,
if those words have gotten inside you,
consider this: it is only right, an echo returning its
clear sound, geese seeking known currents,
a clocktower chiming each night the same pattern of hours.

I am tracing this river back to its source, separating
dancer and dance, unraveling the threads of cello,
harpsichord, violin, bass as the canon spins on. These are
the moments we move through: the sure shades of
spring summer fall to this stark wintered sky.

If we are entering silence, we are entering as
gently as the cup in your hands, gently
as the soft light at the window, the fog over the city,
your sweater tossed on the chair. Words come full
circle: like grapes pressed to wine, deepened by time
they grow lovely and lovelier still.

Keep listening: these measured lines,
learning their places, are really your own.

FALLING INTO GRACE

Washing Dishes

Outside this window, just beyond this glass
is the world: a brilliant jay; a bright-beaked
cardinal and her vivid mate; a handful of tittering chickadees
and a scatter of sparrows.

This is, perhaps, the *why* to why I wash dishes here,
bent over the sink, my knees nearly touching
a machine that would do the task for me. If my
insistence is stubborn, it is not without reason—

the reason being this window and the slant
of morning or evening light—so different—diffuse through the trees.
But years before this scene, I faced white cement block
and I soaked, washed, rinsed in quiet contentment

which means it is not the window but the rhythm, the dance,
dish in—wipe—rinse—dish out like wordless music.
Or perhaps in this act I am connected to generations
of women carrying, heating water and, in pale dusk,

wiping away the remains of one day to prepare for another,
—the cycles of women's time, the turns of their lives.
Washing dishes, arms deep in hot soapy suds,
I know it is this: yes, lovely view of the day and the world;

yes, rhythm and music; yes, link to my mothers. But mostly, this:
the grace of my own act, the slow reclamation as,
plate by cup, knife fork and spoon,
what was unclean is made spotless—

the sacred beneath my slick fingers;
redemption between my wet hands.

103 in November

I met her on a hot July afternoon while canvassing door-to-door for Bible School. I'd walked a long way, my legs were tired, and my arms hurt from carrying the stack of Bibles. Hers was the last house on my road, and I was tempted to skip it and hit the beach. The mailbox read, "J Mitchell" in chipped black paint, its hinges rusty and red flag faded.

The driveway seemed endless. Large trees guarded the silence, hovering over trackless gravel. I paused to shake a stone out of my sandal, swatting at deerflies buzzing in my hair. Then the trees opened to a house. The lawn, newly mown, boasted a thin, dry lilac bush and a clothesline flaunting a tattered wool blanket.

The house stood in the middle of the clearing. Peeling slivers of dull white paint revealed weathered lumber beneath. A small garage gaped open at the end of the drive, empty except for a push mower and a few tools. A narrow cement walk led to the back door, but I started toward the front and crossed the porch cautiously, careful to avoid the loose or missing planks in the floor.

The doorknob rattled when I knocked, and inside a dog yapped and scratched. "Lie down, Butch!" A woman's voice came from behind the door. Then there were hesitant footsteps, the sound of slippers shuffling over linoleum, and the grate of a bolt being slipped from a lock.

The door opened a little, and a wrinkled brown face peered out at me. "Yes, come in," she told me. She moved aside and I stepped in. The room was dark and smelled musty and closed, but as my eyes adjusted I could see we were in a dining room. There was a table near a clouded window, scattered with newspapers and stained with coffee. Beside the table was a large armchair upholstered in patterned plastic and protected by a thin, faded sheet. The woman motioned for me to sit down by the table, then eased herself into the armchair.

I watched her closely, taking in the wispy white hair held to her head by a sheer nylon cap, the hollows around her speckled eyes, the weathered skin folding over her cheeks and jaws. She was bent and crooked in her cotton housedress, and she stared ahead as she spoke.

"I thought you was the health care lady, but you isn't," she said. "My daughter, Nina, she went to town, but she'll be back soon. Soon as the health care lady comes."

The mention of the health care lady made me look around. The wall paper was stained and faded, curling away from the wall near the ceiling.

In the corner of the room behind the woman's chair there was a rope strung between an oil-burning stove and a door leading upstairs. Old, grayed drawers hung from the line, and yellowed newspapers beneath kept water from dripping onto the linoleum.

The woman and I talked then, and she told me how she had farmed the land around the house at one time. "Farmed it all by myself," she told me proudly. "Had chickens and hogs and rabbits and even a cow. But I never had no man here. Just a woman. Just me and my daughter and Butch." She gestured toward the black dog lying on the kitchen floor, his tail wagging rhythmically at the mention of his name.

"My daughter, she takes care of me now," the woman continued. "I don't work no more. Farmed till I was 99—that was three years ago. You know, I'll be 103 in November. So I just stay here." She folded her wrinkled hands, then went on. "Oh, I used to work," she recalled. "Done everything in my life but kill and steal and hurt people. I cooked and cleaned and scrubbed and washed for white folks." She leaned back and sighed. "I even raised their babies. Oh, I loved them babies."

I told her about the kids I was teaching in Bible School, then, and about the summer work we were doing. She replied, "I love to see young people serve the Lord. Cause if you do good, He'll help you in ways you never knew. He gives me breath every morning and I know He's thinking of me. And I know He won't forget me. I don't need nothing but the Lord." She shook her head. "Nothing but the Lord," she repeated, then fell silent.

I waited to hear what she'd say next, but she turned to me and fluttered one hand toward her chest. "The doctor says I shouldn't talk so much—bad for my heart. He says to rest. So much talking ain't good for me, so you better go. But remember, without the Lord you can't do nothing, honey. So you keep serving Him. He's been with me for 102 years, and in November I'll be 103. He's all I got now, and all I need is Him."

She took a deep breath. "You come again. I love you white folks, love you just the same. Cause we're all going to heaven together."

I smiled as I got up to leave, and though I told the woman that I could let myself out, she wanted to lock the door. She pushed herself up from the armchair, and I followed her hesitant footsteps to the door, promising to try to stop again.

As I walked down the shadowed drive to the road, past the lilac, the pines and the mailbox, I realized that she hadn't even told me her name. I knew only that she'd be 103 in November.

First Synod: For Hanna

Knowing there is power in a name,
we called you by one pregnant with the story
of a woman who would not let God go,
a woman whose spirit would not be stilled.
We prayed that same spirit for you.

At four months, I took you
to the "meeting of the brethren"—
a daughter of tomorrow
whose place was the topic of the day.

Those delegates were men of God;
they sang in sweet harmony,
prayed to the Spirit they love
while you slept—
after all, it was not your voice they had come to hear.
It was not mine either, though I, too, am a daughter.

Then the words began.
Voiceless, I had practiced anger,
but my heart was strangely still. Until your cry, clear,
cleaved the quiet. I was swift, but you would not
be silenced. Named for that strong woman,
you made your voice heard.

Flesh of my flesh, bone of my bone,
may that be your first Synod, not your last.
For you reminded us
that you, too, were created in God's image:
eyes, ears, hands and voice—

yes, even voice.

Communion

—to my mother, Room 3207

I am still kneading dough, my hands deep in flour,
when the telephone rings.

Baking bread is my sacrament, a profound act of love:
the smooth stretch of dough, time,

and patience rising within me like yeast.
Still, it is interruptible.

The call says that you've been admitted—you have admitted—
your suffering conceded, pain professed.

I won't phone tonight; I'll give you this night without words
and go back to the bread.

Yet when it is finished, how I wish I could bring you
the warm loaf, fresh from the oven.

I would kneel by your side,
and together our fingers would split the crust wide.

For me: four hundred miles of peace.
For you: grace, the warm center,

and silence to savor the taste of a gift which,
like healing, needs not be spoken.

Refinement

Writing about my mother's MS is a difficult task. How can I pretend to be true in telling whatever I know? My words are those of a daughter, not a writer, and my perceptions are partial at best.

What is hardest for me is beginning: writing for others what we do not say ourselves—not at Christmas, not on birthdays, not before bed, not in front of the children. Timing is everything, and it has never been the right time. Perhaps that time is now; perhaps not.

I want to write about my mother's days, her struggles. I want to say this: hers is the quiet heroism of holding a pen in a hand she has not controlled for years, of tying buttons she cannot feel, of pretending to feel the movement of a grandchild before birth. For in my mother's experience with MS, *feeling* was how it all began—persistent numbness in her hands and feet, tingling, no sensation. At seventeen I was not a very good listener, I was not much of a friend; I wish for her sake I had been more aware of what it all meant. She looked fine, she seemed healthy, and at first there was only a diagnosis by determining what it *wasn't*. It took years before the doctors could tell her with certainty what it *was*. She tired quickly, so our family lived around her need to rest, but we could tolerate that. We were busy with our own lives during those years: dating, college, getting married. So many things were happening and the changes in her life were so gradual. MS was something for the future. MS was never now.

But for her, MS was always now, and only recently have I begun to realize what that means: the grandchildren that grow too heavy too soon, the conversations that are too often cut short, the exhausting effort of each day and each night. And the unpredictability—sometimes headaches, sometimes pain; fatigue that comes and goes, varying degrees of numbness, an uncertain sense of balance. Each time we see her I'm taken by surprise, for her condition can change so much with so little warning. Telephone calls never prepare me; the highs and lows still catch me unaware.

If I had to choose a word to describe the worst part of this disease, I'd probably say loss; my children will know only a part of the woman who raised me, and I will always wish they could know more. We have lost the nurse, the EMT, the woman who canned and froze and gardened, the woman who baked every Saturday and read late into the night and kept an immaculate house. There is no pretending she is the same woman she was; there is no denying some precious things have been lost.

Refinement

But if I had to choose a word to describe the gift that has come through all of this, I would probably say refinement. I keep thinking of the words to that hymn: *"When through fiery trials your pathway shall lie, / my grace all-sufficient shall be your supply; / the flame shall not hurt you; I only design / your dross to consume and your gold to refine."* God has a way of turning sorrow on end, of salvaging loss, and we see that happening in my mother's life. She has gained enormous patience; she has developed a heightened sense of priorities; she demonstrates a great sense of humor; and her faith continues to deepen. Her relationships, especially with her family, are more precious than they would have been fifteen years ago. And if my children will know only part of her, I thank God for showing them the part God loves most.

In writing about MS, this finally is what I must say: MS started out being my mother's disease. Because we love her, it has become all of ours as well.

Six a.m.

This cabin is not the brilliance of flame,
nor the comfort of sky,
but the stain of dried blood, peeling.
No moon's tides or white sands
or nets lined with shimmering scales.

Only a brief beach strewn with stones,
edged with sea's weeds,
and loud gulls circling
the murky ripples of fish that escaped our lures.
This is not the place.

No, not the place—not heaven
or haven or home. But today,
restless dawn brooding,
a slice of warm cinnamon toast
and a mug of black coffee—

today, and this morning, it is enough.

After the Bomb

—April 20, 1995; Oklahoma City

Beneath my clothesline: two tiny sparrows, blue-veined,
sparse feather-fuzzed. Blown, I suppose, from the
tree in last night's storm. The storm
that kept the children awake as thunder
pounded the windows, explosions of sound like a—

It is Thursday, and I can't say it.
I can only hang laundry because I am numb,
because there is comfort in doing what I do and
what I know in the face of all I can't do
and will never understand.

And so with arms raised,
I hang laundry—daughter's pajamas,
son's favorite shirt. The act is serene but my mind is
a sky-piercing *no*—*no* to flames and a silence like
thunder. *No* to camera crews, cranes, and yellow

police tape. *No* to concrete slabs, medic tents,
flags at half mast, *no* to a thousand stitches broken
glass broken bones broken babies *no*
to waiting body bags grief
stories too painful to tell.

No to the sun still rising, the grass still growing,
holly hedge, irises, careless blue sky.
No to mockingbirds, humming birds, cardinal
songs. *No* to finches and gray mourning
doves.

And *no* to the sparrows—the yellow-beaked
sparrows. *No* to the elm tree they fell from.
No to god's eye that was sleeping. And *no*
to the almighty fingers they—hollow-boned, weightless—
slipped through.

outside the funeral home

arms outstretched,
the stained-glass saviour
shines. scarred palms upturned
and lily white, god's
son glows. his robes twist
vivid ribbons in the trees where

blackbirds cringe and
caw at dusk, like dark wet leaves
among bare limbs. restless always, they
imagine foes, taste fear: in flight
their wild wings cast shadows
on the waiting face of christ.

Ash Wednesday

Remember you are dust and to dust you shall return. Repent and believe the Gospel.

Snow is whiter than ash, even cold ash, and Wednesday is the biggest snow of the season—the kind of snow I knew as a child, flakes driven by wind. Because we are children of the snow, we spend the day in it, turning our faces toward heaven to receive the gift on our lashes, tongues, foreheads and cheeks.

Ash is warmer than snow, even cold ash, and at night I bundle the children again and take them to our first Ash Wednesday service, trudging through snow—falling and fallen—to a place of warmth and light. It is comfort I seek; few of us have ventured out, but we are enough. By twos and threes we proceed to the rail, faces upturned to receive the touch of ash pressed to our foreheads.

Remember you are dust and to dust you shall return. I kneel for a blessing but the words feel like ice on my upturned face. When the ash touches my forehead, I feel dust, smell dust, taste dust. It is the touch of my own mortality, yes—I will remember I am dust.

Then the pastor turns to my children. I watch in horror as he makes the sign of the cross on their skin. *Remember you are dust*, he begins. I want to interrupt, to remove the hand from their forehead, the sign from their smooth skin. No, I want to say—*I* may be dust, but *they* are not. They are blood and muscle and bone, grace and laughter, gentleness and flame. They are not dust.

I want to spin them toward me, lick my own fingers and rub and rub the reminder until it is gone. But I let the gray stain stay.

Walking home, the world is snow-quiet, hushed from below and above. We walk in silence; I hold their gloved hands tight in my own. Around us snow covers black earth, red dirt, gray dust and ash. It is like grace, I suppose, on us all—old and young. Falling on our upturned faces. Melting on our foreheads. Insistently washing the ash-gray stains we wear.

Take, Eat, Remember and Believe

Take, eat, remember and believe. In the church of my childhood, communion was something grown-ups did—like driving a car, or going out to dinner, or staying up late at night. It was in the domain of things to be waited for; it was also the domain of "pretend." And pretend we did—not just communion, but all the other rites of passage we observed. Sometimes we pretended the tiny shed on the side of the garage was a beauty shop and we trimmed each other's bangs and tried on the lipstick samples the Avon lady left behind. Sometimes it was the scene for a wedding; sometimes it was a house with a kitchen and a table and chairs; occasionally there was a baby added.

Sometimes, though, we turned the long empty flower planters upside down and set them in straight rows like pews, and the faithful would enter humming the hymns that were part of our youth in a small Calvinist farming town. "Not What My Hands Have Done" was always a good one, and most often I, being oldest, got to be preacher. I was good at it, too—lots of sin and salvation in my messages, climaxing with a round of holy communion passed on discarded Melmac from my mother's kitchen. "Take, eat, remember and believe" I would intone solemnly, passing crackers and dark grape juice. Not a snicker. We knew the part about eating and drinking in an unworthy manner; judgement unto our souls would result—an offense not to be taken lightly, even by a group of six-year-olds.

It amazes me, now, how deeply inscribed those words and phrases were on our child hearts and minds. Those were the days when—and that was the church where—communion was celebrated only four times a year. In our young lives we couldn't have been present for more than a dozen such services, but still we knew the ceremony, we knew what to say, we knew the seriousness such moments deserved.

As the years passed, I grew up into church communion, helping myself to a peppermint from my father's suit coat pocket just as the minister said, "Take, eat." I learned to pass with steady hands the plates of cubed white bread and the heavy trays filled with tiny glasses of grape juice and wine. And, more than a decade later, I took my own first communion at last. Each progressive stage was a thrill, and I decided that some things were indeed worth waiting for. Communion, I concluded, was something you grew into like oversized shoes or the coat you bought ahead for the next winter. When you were big enough, wise enough, good enough, communion would be there, and it would fit.

Take, Eat

Years later, when the sacrament had lost some of its newness but not its thrill, I switched from wine to the grape juice in the center to accommodate my first pregnancy and the birth of a son. Still later, during my years of earth-keeping, I petitioned the church to keep using glass cups instead of disposable plastic; I even washed the tiny glasses after church. During my second pregnancy I belonged to a Lutheran church, which meant that each week I knelt at the rail to receive the elements in my outstretched hand and to take a sip from the common cup, feeling as I knelt the early stirrings of the daughter we named Hanna Grayce. I loved those mornings, when the pastor would face me and whisper, "The body of Christ, given for you" as he handed me the papery wafer and the elder would follow behind with the words, "The blood of Christ, shed for you."

Sometime in those years, though, my son turned three and graduated from nursery to the worship service. I told him a little about it before he sat through his first communion—enough to keep him quiet during the ritual—but afterward he was full of questions. What were we doing and why? I did my best to explain, but how do you say body and blood, sin and salvation to a child? I couldn't. I started to tell him it was a way of reminding ourselves that Jesus had died—no, too abstract. I started to tell him it was a meal we shared with Jesus—no, still too difficult. I fumbled a little, then seized on the simplest and most straightforward response I could give: it's a reminder of how much God loves us. My son thought for a moment—but only a moment—then said, "Shouldn't I be reminded, too? Doesn't God love me?"

It's a question I've asked myself over the years. What is this mystery of communion—holy bread, holy wine, holy people, or holy reminder? Where do crackers and grape juice and children's voices fit in? Where is the thrill of that first taste of the elements? What can I tell my son about a ceremony that surrounds but that does not include him? And what of the year I refused communion, afraid of eating and drinking judgement, once again imagining myself as the wrong size for grace?

It is a full circle I've come, crossing today into the childhood role I so revered, playing out at last the drama begun in the garage shed so long ago. The church that is now my home has lay people assist with communion, stand in front of the congregation and hold the cup of wine. Dozens of people—people I have, over time, learned to know and cherish in various ways—leave their seats, walk to the front, receive bread from the hand of the pastor and dip that bread into the cup—the cup I cradle between my two hands. The pastor says, "The body of Christ, for you," and I say, "Christ's blood that was given for you." It is an odd journey, far from a past where a woman's only service at the communion table was to wash the glasses after the sacrament was over.

Take, Eat

Cup in hand, I look into these peoples' eyes and I know their names. There is an old woman who needs to be helped back to her seat, a couple whose only son is dying of cancer, two teenage brothers who elbow each other as they wait but who stand respectfully before the cup, as if accepting grace and their common blood in the same moment. One woman touches my hand while I speak—as if I am a conduit of sorts, and I suppose I am. I think briefly of the times I refused bread and wine, and as I wonder how God can move through me, I remember the hymn I hummed so often as a child in our make-believe church.

We move toward the piano and the pastor places the juice-soaked bread on the tongue of the organist as she plays—grace in process, without interruption. At the sacrament's close the servers feed one another, an intricate crisscross of pastors and lay people, bread and wine.

But I have not mentioned what is, for me, the most powerful episode of the morning—serving the children. Toddlers in arms, children led, carried, guided into and through the ritual. My own children are there, too. By now this has become part of the rhythm of their worship, part of the story that is theirs. No need for them to dress up or pretend to serve crackers and juice in the back yard. Here, bread and wine belong to them, as to us all. My son is now eight. He meets my eyes with understanding when I tell him Christ's blood is for him. My daughter is three, and as I bend to offer the cup, I say her name. She has no need to ask about God's love; she knows it is hers. She eats and drinks. She remembers and believes.

My Son Asks How I See God

When he asks how I see God,
I slip on the ice hard answers of my childhood,
slide past the white-hot holiness of youth,
into the iridescent folds of this day's
grace.

We are slicing bread, quartering apples
on a bluestone plate. Christmas week;
within the year he will reach my height,
but this afternoon I feel tender, older, wise.
Until his question stuns me with all I cannot describe:
the taste of pomegranate, pine resin, honeysuckle—
each only itself.

Casually, he speaks. *God*, he tells me, *is a cardinal.*
—the cardinal this morning at the feeder,
vivid against the miracle of Oklahoma snow.

I know what he says is true:
the song in the branches is God,
the bright flash from tree to tree, the glint in the evergreens.
Holly berry, mistletoe, icicles dripping from the roof—God.

And I am pleased, here in my kitchen,
to know how he knows, relieved that this is the only flame
he sees in the divine—no all-consuming heat, refining fire;
only a slight steamy exhale

and a quick wing, red-hot against snow.

Jay in a Redbud Tree

It is a bird with wings so blue they are
almost violet

on a branch lined with purple flowers
that are nearly pink

and it is gone before I really know that I have
seen it,

but I have. I know I have.

EPILOGUE

Grace

Water, birds, wind and flame—
they weave through my poems like that
other word: grace.

It is the stone in the creek
that turns smooth flow to foam,

the fringed wing
slicing thin air.

It is breath—not soft breath
but rage of gale, shaping the stark trees,

the hot tongue
refining the story I tell.

So all my words come to this: grace.
I cannot out-run it, out-see,
out-speak, out-write it—

pulse of the universe,
hum in my blood,
center of all my circling:

grace.